Schools' SEN Policies Pack

Coordinated by

Philippa Stobbs, Théresa Mackey, Brahm Norwich
Nick Peacey and Phil Stephenson,

On behalf of

The Council for Disabled Children and East Sussex LEA

The Special Educational Needs Joint Initiative for Training

The Department of Educational Psychology and Special Educational Needs at the
Institute of Education, University of London

and with the support of the Department for Education

Acknowledgements

We wish to acknowledge with grateful thanks all those who have supported the development of this pack by contributing their ideas and by reading, trying out and commenting on materials used in its preparation:

Terry Bailey	Enfield LEA
John Bangs	National Union of Teachers
David Bartlett	Birmingham LEA
Angus Bentley	Education Consultant
Colette Bleakley	West Cheshire College
John Bown	Laycock School, Islington
Virginia Bridge	E. Sussex LEA
Val Buckley	Wandsworth LEA
Ken Campbell	Leeds Social Services
Peter Candlin	St Paul's CE School, East Sussex
Madelaine Caplin	Crown Woods School
Judith Charlesworth	Oakleigh School, Barnet
Hugh Clench	E. Sussex County Psychological Service
Verity Donnelly	Assessment and Curriculum Authority for Wales
Maria Evans	Surrey LEA
Sue Flockton	Barnet LEA
Linda Goldstein	Highgate Wood School, Haringey
Mary Hrekow	Lambeth LEA
Michael Marland	North Westminster School, City of Westminster
Harry Marsh	Contact a Family
Chris Miles	Laycock School, Islington
Gary Nethercott	Essex LEA
Joan Pilkington	E. Sussex LEA
Richard Reiser	Integration Alliance
Philippa Russell	Council for Disabled Children
Christine Salter	Bexley LEA
Tom Shine	Barnet LEA
Jim Smith	Highgate Wood School, Haringey
Neil Smith	Camden LEA
Lyndsey Stone	Barnet LEA
Andy Thomas	Laycock School, Islington
Hazel Underwood	E. Sussex LEA
Phil Weiner	E. Sussex County Psychological Service
Vanessa Wiseman	Langdon School, Newham
Sheila Wolfendale	University of East London
the staff of:	Highgate Wood School, Haringey, Hill Mead Infant School, Lambeth, Langdon School, Newham, St John's Upper Holloway, Islington
schools in:	Barnet, Cambridgeshire, Hackney, East Sussex, Newcastle upon Tyne
teachers in:	Barnet SEN advisory service, the SENJIT ESL/SEN network

representatives of the Association of County Councils, the Association of Metropolitan Authorities and the Society of Education Officers on the Special Needs Advisory Group of the Department for Education, together with Tom Jeffery, Pauline Maddison, Martin Sharpe, Terry Bailess and colleagues of the Department for Education and Chris Marshall and Diane Chorley of the Office for Standards in Education. We also acknowledge with grateful thanks the help of Val Bull and Fiona Blakemore in the preparation of this pack.

ISBN 1 874579 41 5
Published by National Children's Bureau Enterprises Ltd, 8 Wakley Street, London EC1V 7QE.
The National Children's Bureau is a registered charity, number 258825
Typeset by Futura Printing Limited, London. Printed by Greenshires Print Limited, Kettering, Northamptonshire.

The photograph is Crown copyright and permission for its use has been granted by the Department for Education. The National Children's Bureau gratefully acknowledges the parents, teachers and children of Wheatley Park School, Oxford for permission to use the photograph.

Foreword

This pack has been designed to support schools in developing their SEN policy. The materials are intended as a resource for schools to draw upon as needed. The starting point of the pack is the main review document which is designed to help schools to identify their own priorities and to select the most relevant units for their use. The units within the pack have not been designed to be read and used one after the other.

Similarly, within each unit, and following the more detailed review, schools can select which parts of that unit they use. In addition they can draw on relevant discussion papers where they think these may helpfully inform their deliberations and their proposed developments. The purpose of the discussion papers is to access schools to a wide range of current issues, ideas and developments in the special needs field.

Different schools will find different parts of the pack more relevant and more useful for their purposes and other parts less so. Our assumption is that no two schools will use the pack in the same way. We hope that over time schools will return to it and find useful parts of the pack that they didn't stop to visit the first time around.

The materials are intended for mainstream primary and secondary schools, though there are sections that will also be relevant to special schools, pupil referral units and nursery schools. Schools have contributed significantly to the development of this pack. We hope it will prove to be a useful resource to the schools using it.

The coordinators

Philippa Stobbs is Senior Development Officer, Council for Disabled Children.

Théresa Mackey is Adviser for SEN, East Sussex LEA.

Brahm Norwich is Senior Lecturer, Department of Educational Psychology and Special Educational Needs, Institute of Education, University of London.

Nick Peacey is Coordinator, Special Educational Needs Joint Initiative for Training, Institute of Education, University of London.

Phil Stephenson is Advisory teacher for SEN, East Sussex LEA.

Unit 1: Guide to using the pack

Schools' SEN policies pack
Using the materials

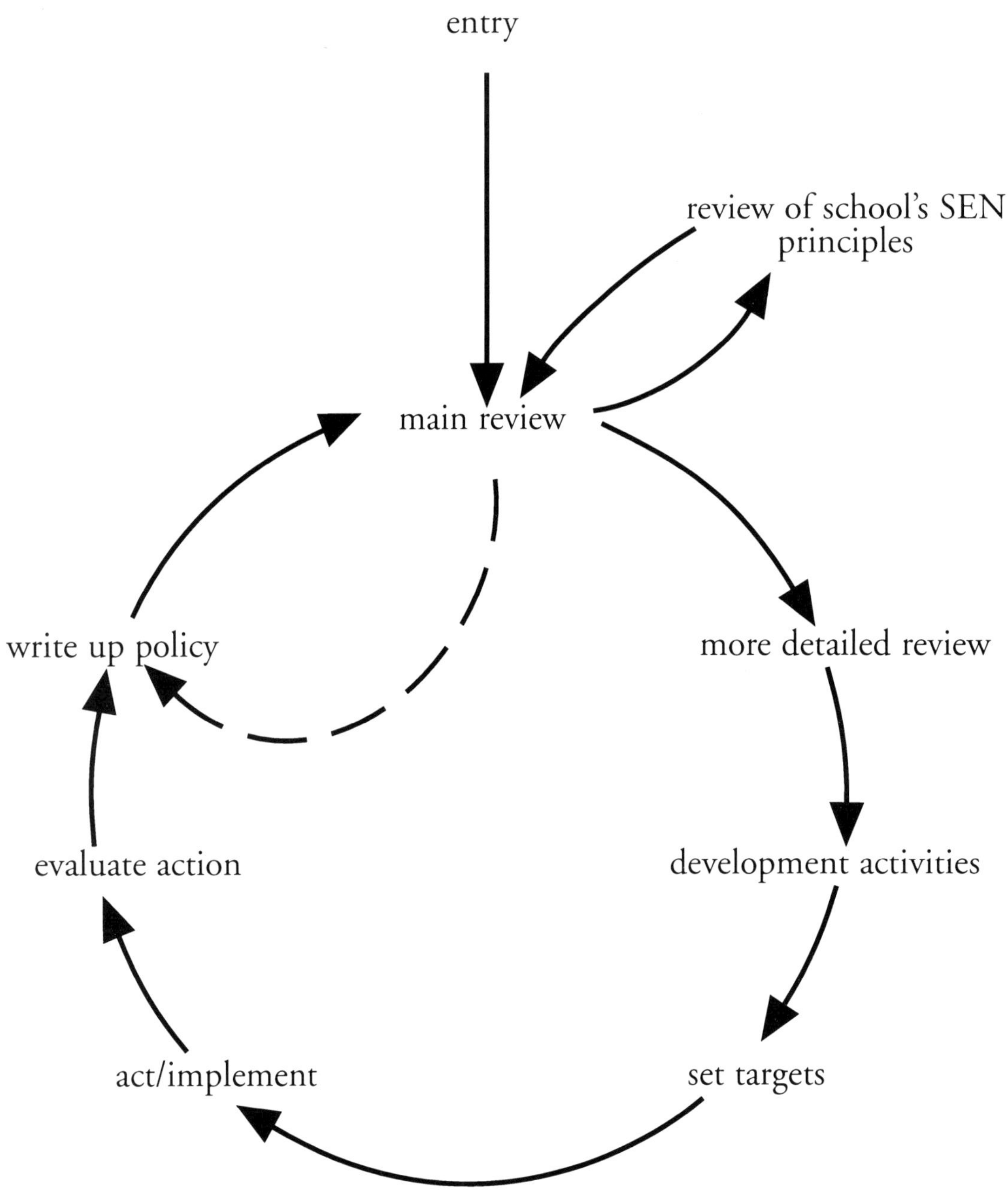

Schools' SEN policies pack

This pack has been designed to support schools in developing their SEN policies. It can be used in a number of different ways:

- to help schools to write up their existing policy to meet the requirements of the Regulations;
- to assist schools in the systematic review of their SEN policy and practice;
- to provide materials for staff development and in-service training on meeting SEN;
- to support the longer term development of SEN policy and practice through school development planning.

The pack is organised in fourteen units and a collection of discussion papers:

Unit 1: Guide to using the pack

This guides the reader on how to use the pack, how to organise the review and development work in school and how to write up the policy. At the centre of this unit is the main review document. This will be the starting point for most schools using the pack.

Units 2 - 13 focus on:

2. Values and principles
3. Identification, assessment and review
4. Access to the curriculum
5. Roles and responsibilities
6. Staff development
7. Admissions, facilities, specialisms and integration
8. Allocation of resources
9. Parent involvement
10. Support services and other schools
11. Transfer and transition
12. Working with other agencies
13. Monitoring and evaluation

These units reflect the different elements in the Regulations on Schools' SEN policies: the Education (Special Educational Needs) (Information) Regulations 1994. It is not necessary or even desirable to work on more than one unit at a time. Schools can use the main review in Unit 1 to help them decide which unit they want to work on. Each of these units contains:

- a more detailed review;
- a range of staff development activities;
- materials to support the development activities;
- reference to other supportive documents.

Unit 14 provides a summary of the contents of the rest of the pack.

Discussion papers:

There is a collection of discussion papers in a series of five companion volumes.

Contents

Structure of the pack 11

The aims of the pack and some underlying assumptions 13

The general approach 17

How the pack is organised 21

The framework for schools 25

The legislative framework 27

The governors and the school's SEN policy 29

Organising the work in school 33

SEN and school development planning 37

The main review: questions to support school self-review 43

Introduction 45

The main review 47

Setting priorities for development 60

Writing up the school's SEN policy 63

Introduction 65

What has to be in the school's SEN policy 67

Support materials 77

Further reading 93

Structure of the pack

Contents

The aims of the pack and some underlying assumptions	13
The general approach	17
How the pack is organised	21

The aims of the pack and some underlying assumptions

The Schools' SEN Policies Pack has been developed to:

- support schools in writing up their SEN policy in line with the requirements of the Education (Special Educational Needs) (Information) Regulations 1994;
- help schools to 'have regard to' the Code of Practice;
- be of continuing use to schools in reviewing and developing their SEN policy and practice;
- provide a framework for setting SEN priorities within the context of the school's development plan.

Many schools already have a policy on SEN. This pack aims to help schools to develop their policy whether they already have one or not, and regardless of its current state of development. The pack is based on these assumptions:

Schools and policies change

Schools develop and change and so do their policies. Thus the school's published policy at a particular time is assumed to be a snap-shot of the school at that time. As the school's policy and practice develop the written documentation needs to reflect the changes.

Policy and practice develop over time

Schools will be developing policy and practice over time in a systematic way. The pack offers help with:

- setting priorities;
- putting the tasks in order;
- making the process manageable.

SEN policy and practice is best developed within the school development plan

The development of the pack has been informed by work done in schools on development planning, and also by our understanding of effective, self-managing schools. Schools that will benefit most from using this pack will be those that have an awareness and some understanding of this approach. This is fully discussed in the section in this unit on SEN and school development planning, see page 37. There is encouragement to schools to adopt this approach in Circular 6/94:

> *'Schools' SEN policies should be an integral part of the school's strategic planning. There will often, for example, be links between schools' SEN policies and their behaviour policies. Schools may therefore wish to incorporate the development of their SEN policies into the school development plans.'*

The requirements of the legislation will clearly make SEN a high priority within the development plan of most schools.

SEN developments are integral to and dependent on other developments but also have a distinct identity

SEN policy and practice touch on almost every area of the school's endeavour, so care is taken to relate SEN to existing policy and practice in other areas. These issues are also explored in the section in this unit on SEN and school development planning, see page 37.

Everyone in the school will be involved in some way

Everyone at the school is involved with SEN policy and practice:

> *'The governing body and the head teacher will take overall responsibility for developing and implementing the school's SEN policy. But the school as a whole should be involved and schools may wish to consult neighbouring schools, the local education authority and, as appropriate, the Funding Agency for Schools (FAS). Schools may also find it helpful to consult parents. Before reporting annually to parents, schools may wish to consult any external specialists who have worked closely with them over the past year.'*
>
> paragraph 27 of Circular 6/94

The school's best endeavours to meet SEN involve everyone at the school: class and subject teachers and all support staff, those with pastoral responsibility, curriculum leaders, the SEN coordinator, the head teacher and senior managers and the governors. In turn, the school's SEN policy will affect the way that everyone works within the school and the way in which they work with those outside the school. However, the particular way in which the review and development work is carried out will vary widely from school to school. The pack supports schools in deciding how best to approach the task in their particular setting including whether or not they may wish to involve outside agencies in the process.

Schools will use the pack in different ways according to their particular purposes

The way in which SEN policy will be developed will vary from school to school. Schools may want to use the pack to:

- write up their policy:

  in which case schools will need to refer directly to the section: Writing up the school's SEN policy. From this section schools may want to refer to other units in the pack;

- review their SEN policy and practice:
  in which case schools may want to use the review document. Again, from this point, they may want to refer to other units in the pack;

- support development work in a particular area:
  in which case the school may want to use one particular unit;

- use selected development activities to support general staff development on SEN:
  in which case schools may want to draw on the development activities in the different units;

- use the structure of the pack to support the longer term development of SEN policy and practice:
  in which case schools may want to work through the pack in a more systematic way, drawing on the different units to help meet development priorities.

Our intention is that the materials should support schools in reviewing their current policy and practice, in identifying development needs, addressing these needs, and drawing up, implementing and monitoring action plans to meet these needs. Schools are also guided through writing up their policy and procedure in the areas on which they are statutorily required to report in their published policy. Schools are supported in considering how to evaluate the effectiveness of their policy. How the school conducts this evaluation is in itself one of the areas on which the school has to publish its policy.

The school's published SEN policy document will be short

The school's agreed policy will be short, perhaps four or five pages, and refer to detailed plans and related policies where appropriate. This issue is considered further in the section: Writing up the school's SEN policy.

The general approach

Schools may use this pack in a number of different ways. These are considered in the previous section on page 14. The materials have been designed to support schools in linking the review and development of their SEN policy and practice to their development plan. This process is outlined below.

Using the pack

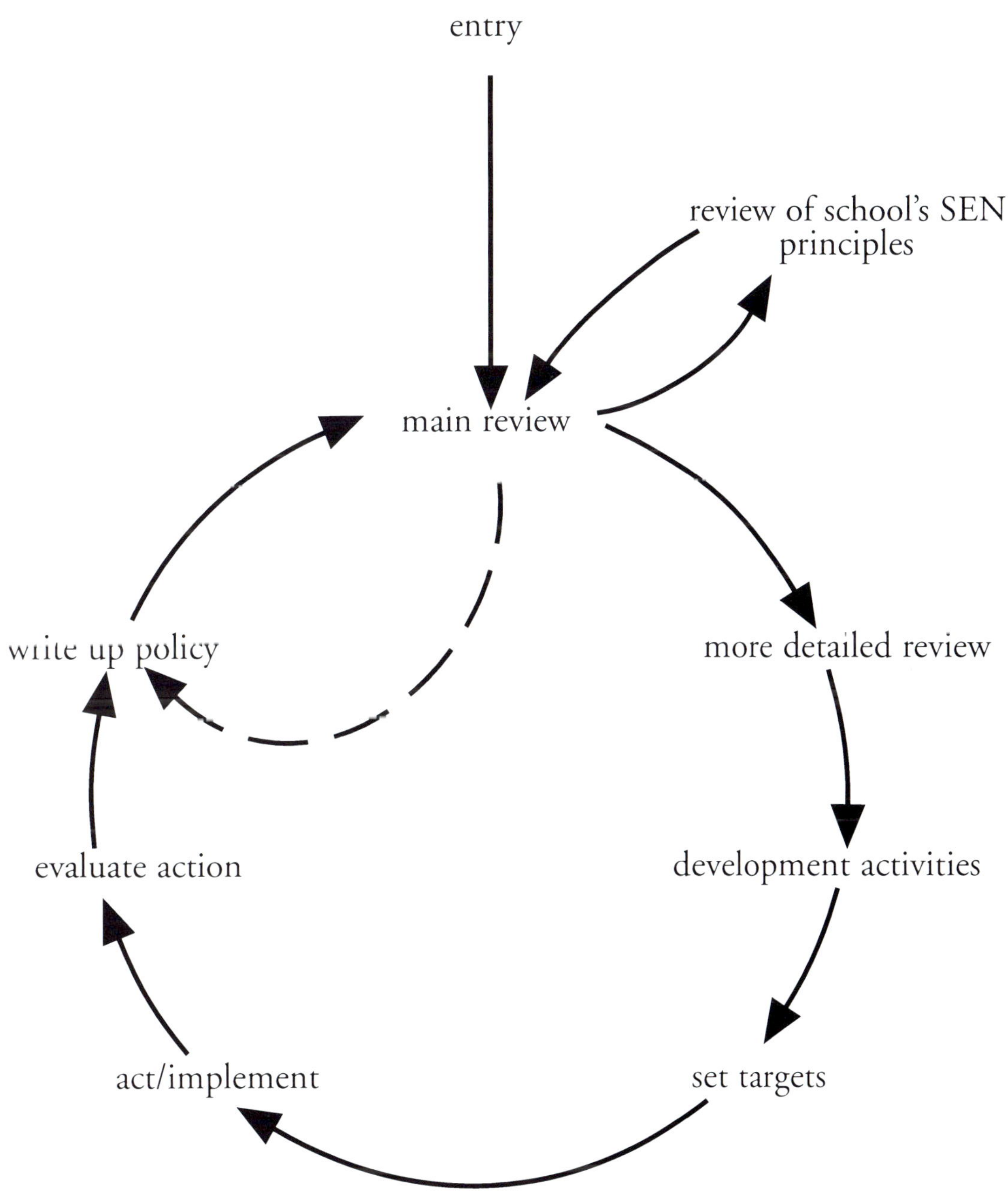

Brief outline of stages of process

The above model outlines in broad stages the progression involved in development planning. It is important to remember that movement forward does not usually take a simple step by step path.

Main review

The process starts with the main review, see page 47. The review assesses in broad terms the school's current policies and practices on SEN and takes careful account of the way in which these dovetail with the school's policies and practices in other areas. The school will need to plan how the review is going to be conducted. There is some guidance on how the work might be organised on page 33.

Setting priorities for development

Out of this review it may emerge that the school lacks a clear set of principles to guide the development of its special educational provision. If this is the case the school would need to address this aspect of the school's policy first.

Carrying out the main review will highlight to the school the areas of policy and practice that need further development. The school then needs to decide which of these areas should be addressed as a short term goal, and which should be built into the school's development plan as longer term goals. There is a number of factors to be taken into account when setting priorities for development. These include a consideration of current priorities for the school's general development and targets already within the school development plan; the size, scope and logical sequence of any areas for development; the potential for linking different developments together; and not least, the need to meet the SEN requirements. Some guidance on this is provided on page 60.

The more detailed review of different areas of the school's SEN policy

Having decided on the priority area for immediate development, the school then turns to the relevant unit within the pack. Each of units 2-13 addresses a different aspect of the school's SEN policy and practice. Within each unit the starting point is a more detailed review. It may be that the school chooses to undertake more than one detailed review at a time, but careful consideration must be given to the setting of realistic, manageable targets within an agreed time-scale. The more detailed reviews will give indications of specific areas for further development.

The development work

The pack then provides some activities which can be used as starting points for schools' development work in this area. Following each activity, schools are provided with a set of questions or issues designed to support them in setting targets for the work that needs to be done next. The time is then ready to implement these specific plans.

Monitoring and evaluating the process

The action/implementation stage is then monitored and finally there is an evaluation of the process and outcomes. The last development activity in each of the units will help the school in this.

Writing up the SEN policy

The agreed principles and procedures in the particular area of the review, for example parent involvement, can then be written up to form the relevant component of the SEN policy. Guidance on this is provided on page 63 of this unit.

Revisiting the review

As part of the annual cycle of review, development, implementation, evaluation and reporting, the school will then return to the main review. Returning to the review will help the school in drawing up the annual report on the implementation of the SEN policy.

How the pack is organised

The pack consists of 14 units and a collection of discussion papers:

1. Guide to using the pack (GD) *
2. Values and principles (V&P)
3. Identification, assessment and review (IAR)
4. Access to the curriculum (AC)
5. Roles and responsibilities (R&R)
6. Staff development (SD)
7. Admissions, facilities, specialisms and integration (AFSI)
8. Allocation of resources (AOR)
9. Parent involvement (PIN)
10. Support services and other schools (SSOS)
11. Transfer and transition (T&T)
12. Working with other agencies (WOA)
13. Monitoring and evaluation (M&E)
14. Summary of contents

*The support materials in the pack are coded according to the unit to which they belong. The code for each unit appears in brackets beside it.

Unit 1: Guide to using the pack

This introductory unit sets out the rationale for the pack, describes how to use it, and includes the main review document which will be the starting point for most schools. The contents page provides a guide to the location of the various sections.

Units 2-13: the units covering the different elements of the school's SEN policy

The organisation of the units broadly reflects the different elements in the Regulations on schools' SEN policies: the Education (Special Educational Needs) (Information) Regulations 1994. There is some grouping of these elements into the different areas covered by the units. The precise relationship between the Regulations and the units is set out in the section: Writing up the school's SEN policy.

None of the units addresses a discrete set of issues. This reflects the fact that the different elements of the school's policy and practice are interwoven with each other in a variety of ways. Thus the values and principles which underpin the whole of the school's work on SEN are an integral part of each area and inform the school's policy and practice in each area. The school's work on monitoring and evaluating its provision is also threaded through each area and is itself closely related to the values and principles which need to provide a framework for monitoring and evaluation.

Other areas are closely related to each other. So, for example, the way in which roles and responsibilities are organised within the school will be one of the most significant factors in determining the allocation of resources to work with children with SEN; and the way in which teaching and learning is organised within the classroom will have a significant impact on the extent to which children with SEN can be integrated with their peers.

There are also themes which weave through the different areas of the pack. Thus, pupil involvement which is one of the principles underpinning the Code of Practice is considered in a variety of ways within a number of different areas though it is not addressed in a separate unit.

As well as being closely related to each other, each of the aspects of the school's SEN policy and practice is closely related to policy and practice in that area for all children. This issue is addressed in the section on SEN school development planning on page 37 of this unit. So, for instance, the school's policy on assessment for children with SEN will be an extension of the school's policy on assessment for all children. Similarly, the way in which the school manages children with emotional and behavioural difficulties will be an extension of the school's approach to behaviour for all children, or the school's IT policy will affect the access to learning resources for all pupils as well as those with learning difficulties and disabilities. In addition, the more comprehensive and the more effective the school's policy and practice for all children, the less the school will need additional measures for children with SEN. We return to this issue in the section: Writing up the school's SEN policy.

Despite this inter-relation, the work clearly has to be divided up to make it manageable. The particular way in which the pack is divided up is dictated largely by the elements in the Regulations on schools' SEN policies. The focus of each unit is clear. However, there are no boundaries around each of the units, we cross refer between units, and schools may want to use materials from one unit in support of work in a different area.

Structure of the units

Each of the units is organised in the same way and contains:

- an introduction;
- review questions;
- development activities;
- materials to support the development activities;
- suggestions for further reading.

The introduction

The introduction briefly summarises the key issues that are addressed in that unit, and that will be picked up as themes in the review, in the development activities and in the relevant discussion papers.

The review questions

The review provides some questions that schools may want to ask of themselves on that aspect of policy and practice. The review within each unit provides a more detailed version of the questions that are asked in the main review. Schools can use the review in the way that best suits their purposes, but it need not be a protracted exercise. It is possible to go through the review fairly quickly and identify the development priorities for the school.

The development activities

The development activities are designed to provide schools with a series of starting points for development work on that particular aspect of policy and practice. Within each unit the first development activity is designed to help schools plan their work in that area, drawing on the pack and on other ideas to meet the development needs that they have identified through using the review. Most of the activities are designed to be undertaken as part of a staff training session. After each development activity schools are asked to record their decisions and set targets for subsequent action agreeing who is responsible for doing what and within what timescale.

Towards the end of the work in each unit, schools are asked to take stock of their progress and to check which targets have been achieved and which have not.

Support materials

In this section there are materials that schools may wish to draw on when they undertake the development activities in the pack. In addition, there are relevant sections of the Code of Practice reproduced in a photocopiable form. These can be used to support development work that schools design for themselves.

The support materials are coded according to the unit to which they belong. So, for example, all the support materials in this Unit: Guide to using the pack, are coded GD, those in Unit 2: Values and principles, are coded V&P, and so on.

Further reading

At the end of each unit we provide a list of books and other materials that may be helpful if schools want to develop their work in this area in greater detail.

Unit 14: Summary of contents

Unit 14 provides a summary of the contents of all the other units. Since none of the areas of the school's SEN policy and practice can be considered as a discrete area, schools may want to draw on activities and materials from other units. This unit sets out where all the discussion papers and the other support materials are located.

Discussion papers

In a series of five companion volumes there is a collection of discussion papers. Each discussion paper provides a personal perspective on some of the issues which are at the heart of the different units.

The discussion papers in no way represent a set of instructions for schools but rather they provide a range of insights which are intended to inform and stimulate the discussion of the issues within the school and to support the school in identifying positive ways forward. As such they can be drawn upon at any point in the process where they may be relevant.

The views expressed in *all* the discussion papers are those of the authors concerned, and do not necessarily reflect the views of the Department for Education.

The framework for schools

Contents

The legislative framework	27
The governors and the school's SEN policy	29
Organising the work in school	33
SEN and school development planning	37

The legislative framework

Part III of the Education Act 1993, the Code of Practice on the identification and assessment of SEN and the associated Regulations and guidance provide a comprehensive new framework for working with children and young people with SEN. This is a framework within which schools, LEAs, health and social services and voluntary organisations all have a part to play in responding effectively to children's SEN. The response of the different agencies is the more effective where they work closely with each other and with parents. These principles underlie the guidance set out in the Code of Practice.

Schools and the Education Act 1993

The duties in the 1993 Act and the principles of the Code of Practice have their origins in the 1981 Act. Significant duties on schools are carried forward from the 1981 Act to Part III of the 1993 Act. Schools are required:

- to use their 'best endeavours' on behalf of children with SEN; and
- to integrate children with SEN with their peers for as much of the time as is 'reasonably practicable'.

In addition to these long-standing duties there are additional duties for schools under Part III of the 1993 Act. Most significantly:

- from 1 September 1994 schools have to 'have regard to' the Code of Practice whenever they make decisions about how to provide for children with SEN;
- by 1 August 1995 schools must publish their SEN policy covering the areas set out in the Regulations;
- thereafter the governing body is required to report on the implementation and the development of that policy in their annual report to parents;
- in carrying out their duties towards pupils with SEN they must consult other parties to the extent that it appears necessary or desirable for the purpose of coordinating provision for pupils with SEN.

The purpose of this pack is to support schools in meeting their new duties in respect of their SEN policy. For many schools the most pressing requirement will be to publish their policy by 1 August 1995. However, the foreword to the Code of Practice recognises that the impact of the Code and of the schools' SEN policies requirements will develop over time. It is not expected that schools will have fully developed every element of their SEN policy by 1 August 1995. The Foreword to the Code of Practice is helpful in acknowledging this. In fact, the initial policy published may simply note for some areas 'This area will be fully examined in 1995-6 (or 1996-7)'. Schools will want to demonstrate to OFSTED and other monitoring agencies a systematic - not a rushed - approach to policy making in SEN. The pack aims to support schools in meeting the immediate requirements and in managing the longer term review and development of policy and practice.

The pack draws on the guidance in the Code of Practice and Circular 6/94 and the Regulations on schools' SEN policies. Some materials are drawn from these documents and are reproduced in different units in this pack. This is in order to make them available in photocopiable form for the purpose of supporting staff development activities.

In working with the materials in this pack it will however be assumed that schools have available these key documents:

- the Code of Practice on the identification and assessment of SEN, and the Education (Special Educational Needs) Regulations 1994 - these are published at the back of the Code of Practice;
- Circular 6/94: the Organisation of Special Educational Provision, and the Education (Special Educational Needs) (Information) Regulations 1994 which are the Regulations on schools' SEN policies and are published at the back of Circular 6/94;
- the pack of six Circulars 'Pupils with Problems':

  8/94: Pupil Behaviour and Discipline;

  9/94: the Education of Children with Emotional and Behavioural Difficulties;

  10/94: Exclusions from School;

  11/94: the Education by LEAs of Children Otherwise Than at School;

  12/94: the Education of Sick Children;

  13/94: the Education of Children Being Looked After by Local Authorities.

These documents have been sent to every school. Further copies of the Code and the Circulars are available, free of charge, by telephoning: 0181-533-2000.

The governors and the school's SEN policy

The Code of Practice sets out the responsibilities of the governing body, 2:6. A copy of this can be found on sheet GD2, page 80 of the support materials.

The responsibility for the school's SEN policy lies with the governing body. The Code, 2:7, indicates that governors should:

> *'in cooperation with the head teacher, determine the school's general policy and approach to provision for children with SEN, establish the appropriate staffing and funding arrangements and maintain a general oversight of the school's work.'*

Paragraph 6 of Circular 6/94 reinforces this statement and clarifies the duties of the head teacher in relation to the governing body.

Section 161(5) of the 1993 Education Act states that the governing body must report on the implementation and effectiveness of the school's policy for pupils with SEN in their annual report to parents.

A table of responsibilities for SEN policy, based on the above documents, looks like this:

School's SEN Policy	Responsibility
Policy determination	governors in cooperation with head teacher
Establishment of appropriate staffing	governors in cooperation with head teacher
Monitoring work on SEN	governors in cooperation with head teacher
Day to day management	head teacher keeping the governors informed
Day to day operation	SEN coordinator
Reporting on policy	governors

Oversight and monitoring: possible arrangements

A nominated SEN governor

Some governing bodies have nominated a governor to take a particular interest in SEN and in some schools this works well.

During the passage of the 1993 Act through Parliament there was considerable pressure on the government to enshrine this arrangement in legislation and to require schools to appoint a governor with expertise in and experience of SEN. This governor would take a special interest in this area of the school's work. This pressure was resisted for several reasons, not least among them the risk that SEN might be seen to be the responsibility of that governor alone, whereas in reality the responsibility lies with the entire governing body.

An SEN committee of the governing body

There is some encouragement in the Code for the governing body to appoint:

> *'a committee to take a particular interest in and closely monitor the school's work on behalf of children with special educational needs.'*

Such an arrangement may better reflect the corporate nature of the governors' responsibilities.

SEN subsumed into the work of the curriculum committee

Another possibility, which works well for some governing bodies, is to include the SEN interest within the brief of the governors' curriculum committee. This has the advantage of including work on SEN at the centre of oversight of teaching and learning in the school.

Oversight and monitoring: the groundwork

This pack sets the work on the school's SEN policy firmly within the context of school development planning. The governors have a key role in decisions about the school development plan and the allocation of the resources to meet the priorities within the plan. The governors' oversight of the development of the school's SEN policy will thus sit alongside their oversight of the school development plan.

The governors need to consider carefully how they achieve oversight of the school's SEN policy.

Awareness

The first requirement will be that they become familiar with the implications of Part III of the 1993 Act, the Code of Practice, the Regulations and Circular 6/94. To this end, they may want to take advantage of training that may be available locally through the LEA or from other agencies. (See discussion paper by Nick Peacey: Special educational needs and staff development in school, in Discussion Papers: II.)

Review

The main review document in this pack, see page 47 of this booklet, enables governors, in cooperation with the head teacher, to carry out a preliminary examination of the current situation.

Completion of the main review will lead to the identification of areas of policy and practice needing further work. These can then be prioritised and fitted into a schedule that allows appropriate resourcing for the work.

As each area of the review is completed, development priorities will become apparent.

Development priorities

The governors will need to consider with the head teacher the development priorities arising from the review and decide:

- how any immediate development needs are going to be addressed;

- within what time scale;
- who is going to lead the work;
- what resources will need to be allocated to the work;
- which development needs will be addressed in the medium and in the long term;
- what adjustments may need to be made to the school development plan to incorporate the proposed SEN developments.

Writing up the policy

The governors will need to ensure that there are arrangements in place for the writing up of the SEN policy.

Continuing oversight

The governors will need to exercise continuing oversight of the SEN policy. The governors might want to consider:

- a regular SEN item on the agenda at meetings of the governing body;
- regular reports from the head teacher on different aspects of the school's provision for pupils with SEN;
- appropriate statistical information on special needs provision, for example, the number of pupils at Stages 1, 2, 3, 4 and 5;
- governor representation on any steering group set up to lead the work of the school on SEN;
- a committee of the governing body to monitor the school's work on SEN;
- a combination of some of the above.

Subsequent reviews of the policy

The governors will need to set in place arrangements for the review of the school's SEN policy in order to be able to report on it in their annual report to parents.

The governors may want to use parts of this pack to explore the issues in the school's work on SEN. This section of the pack is designed for governors, other parts of the pack may usefully inform governors. Governors may want to use the more detailed reviews within the units in the pack to guide their consideration of different aspects of the school's SEN provision. They may want to adapt particular development activities for their own use or to read some of the discussion papers in order to explore particular sets of issues or views about SEN policy and practice.

Organising the work in school

The school may choose to organise the review and development work on SEN policy and practice in a variety of ways. The approach adopted by the school will be determined in part at least by the size of the school and the complexity of its organisation.

However the school chooses to organise the work, there are some key principles that we believe will contribute significantly to the overall effectiveness of the school's work:

- the work should be overseen by the governors and the head teacher;
- the work should draw on the wider community to the maximum extent possible;
- the work should involve all the staff at the school.

The work should be overseen by the governors and the head teacher. The reasons for this are as follows:

- in the legislation responsibility for the school's policy lies with the governing body;
- responsibility needs to be at this level in order to link it to the school's longer term strategic planning processes;
- responsibility needs to be at this level in order to be able to draw on the necessary human and financial resources to support the work;
- responsibility needs to be at this level in order to secure the coordination of the work across different areas of the school; and
- ultimately the whole school will need to operate the policy and therefore commitment to it needs to come from the most senior level.

The work should draw on the wider community to the maximum extent possible. The views of parents, of those involved in supporting the school in their work, of teaching support services, of educational psychology and educational welfare services, of other LEA-based services and of other agencies will helpfully inform decisions about the development of the school's approach. Schools may want to consult the named person of any pupil with a statement, local voluntary organisations and disabled people's organisations. There will be particular aspects of policy and practice where the school will want to consult with other schools and the LEA for the purpose of the coordination of special educational provision in the area.

The involvement of the wider community in the review and development of SEN policy and practice will help to secure their commitment to supporting the school in implementing any changes. For the same reasons the school will benefit from the involvement of pupils themselves in considering the school's special educational provision.

The work should involve all the staff at the school. This third principle is related to the first in that ultimately the whole staff will be involved in the operation of the policy and therefore they need to be involved in its development. These three principles should inform the management of the work on SEN policy and practice, but the detail of the way it is organised will vary widely from school to school. For instance, in a single-form entry primary school it may be that most of the staff are involved in most of the work for most of the time. Whereas in a large secondary school it may be more effective to have a steering group to support the head teacher in organising the work in the school. This group can then involve different staff at different stages, and all staff at some stages.

Setting up a steering group

Where a steering group is drawn together for this purpose there are some important considerations to be borne in mind about how such a group is selected. We set out below some of the drawbacks and some of the benefits of particular approaches to the selection of the steering group.

A self-selected group:

The potential drawbacks of a self-selected group are that:

- the group may not be representative of the full range of the school's work across curriculum areas and the age of pupils taught, or of the level of responsibility and experience of members of staff;
- such a group may be like-minded and therefore not incorporate the diversity of views there may be amongst the staff;
- there may therefore be an increased risk that other staff might dismiss the work of the group.

The potential benefits are that such a group is:

- well-motivated;
- able to maintain the impetus of the work.

A representative group:

If a group is selected to represent a variety of perspectives across the curriculum and the age-range taught and the level of responsibility and experience of members of staff there may nonetheless be drawbacks:

- the group may not be so highly motivated;
- there may be a greater diversity of views.

There are, however, potential benefits. These are that:

- the work is more likely to have an impact across the school;
- the status of the work will be higher;
- diversity of views may be turned to good effect in promoting the debate about ways of developing policy and practice.

In thinking about who may need to be on a steering group it will be important to think about a range of interests:

- how should non-teaching staff be represented?
- should non-staff governors be represented on the group?

Planning the work and who will do it

Whether or not the school decides to use a steering group and whatever the final composition of any steering group, there will need to be agreement about who will be involved at the different stages of the work, and about the time-scale for the work. It may help to look at the different stages outlined in the section: The general approach, see page 17, and write down against each stage:

- who will lead the work;
- who will be involved;
- the proposed timescale for the work.

SEN and school development planning

The considerable developments in the educational provision for pupils with special educational needs in ordinary schools since the 1981 Education Act have been based on the principles of whole school planning and a commitment to cross-school SEN policies and practices. These developments are being reinforced and could be enhanced with the introduction of the Code of Practice. The intention of this pack is to link the new requirement for schools to draw up and report on their SEN policy with a means of doing this through school development planning.

The school's SEN policy has to include information about the guiding principles which inform the school's provision and the objectives which their SEN policy seeks to secure. Schools are also required to report annually on the implementation of their SEN policy. This means that drawing up a policy is connected directly with development plans to enhance provision for pupils with SEN.

The approach taken in this pack is that schools will link their policy reporting with the process of implementing it through school development planning.

School development planning

School development planning, also known sometimes as school review and development, has become a central feature of attempts to enhance school provision in response to changing needs and major national educational initiatives. There are several well-known approaches which will be familiar to many teachers and it is not intended to concentrate on the different emphasis of these systematic attempts to enable school change (the section: Further reading, on page 93 includes some relevant materials).

There are some key elements which are common to all of these approaches:

- an assessment based on data and an analysis of the school's practices, strengths and weaknesses;
- an identification of the priorities for development through a process which takes account of a wide range of views and values;
- the design of development plans in terms of outcomes and routes to them, taking account of resource considerations;
- the formulation of action plans which are specific about success criteria, timing and responsibilities;
- the need for consultation with interested parties and endorsement for the plans;
- monitoring the implementation and progress towards planned goals.

Much of the advice about school development planning places an emphasis on rational planning along the lines outlined above. These approaches are most useful in providing clear guidance about the direction of planning and steering the management of change. However, they can sometimes not take account of the social and organisational realities of schools in which there are differing perspectives and interests which interact in the assessment of needs, setting priorities, and designing and implementing plans. In view of the fact that SEN has been an aspect for which outside systems have taken responsibility, it is especially important to take account of the micro-politics of schools in development planning from an SEN perspective. This means that planning schemes like the one outlined below need to be used in the context of an understanding of the differing perspectives and interests within schools.

Points to remember about the change process

Much has been learned about educational change over recent years which has relevance to school SEN developments. Change is a process, an uneven and unpredictable one, and not an event. Much of the change is technically simple but complex socially in that it involves professionals working in complex organisations. Educational change can be seen, as Fullan[1] does, as a learning experience for the adults involved. It is therefore associated with uncertainties, resistances and challenges. Some schools are better prepared than others for undertaking the change process, and some schools are located in LEAs which are better prepared to support the change process.

The processes of initiating and implementing the change process are critical to school development planning. Initiation is more likely to arise when the change is seen as relevant to the needs of the school. Changes which are practical, clear and meet needs are more likely to be initiated. Also, it is important whether the school has the capacity, both practical and conceptual, to initiate and adopt a development unless there are the resources, both human and financial, to support the change process. Implementation is also more likely to occur when the proposed change relates to perceived needs. But, this has to be seen in the context of the heavy agendas which schools have for change. This has especial relevance to the question of SEN developments and the tendency for this aspect of development to take lower priority. Whether this happens also depends on the clarity and complexity of the developments being implemented. Significant SEN developments depend on developments in other crucial areas of a school's functioning - such as assessment, behaviour management, classroom management and teaching. This can increase the complexity of SEN developments and lead to a lack of clarity over development goals and approaches. SEN developments therefore depend on an understanding of how these developments relate to and depend on developments in other areas of a school. What is required is an appreciation of the complexity of this task and the balancing of such complexity with the need for clarity of ends and means.

What is special about school development planning from a SEN perspective?

SEN, like other aspects of education such as Personal and Social Education, is a cross-school and cross-curricular aspect of education. For this reason SEN development planning cannot be isolated and worked on without bringing in other critical parts of a school's policy and practice. However, SEN aspects of a school and their development also need to be considered as having a distinct identity. Without this identity there is a serious risk that the interests of those with difficulties in learning may become submerged by the interests of the majority.

This assumption that SEN developments are integral to and dependent on other developments *but* also have a distinct identity is the basis of the approach adopted in this pack.

This dependence of SEN developments on other aspects of a school's functioning and developments has significant implications for thinking about and planning school developments from a SEN perspective.

Distinct and integral aspects of school developments from an SEN aspect

School development planning usually involves setting priorities for specific areas for development. In identifying specific areas there is always the risk of forgetting that each specific area is related to other areas and considerations. Separating out specific areas makes for a more manageable development task. However, it has the disadvantage of overlooking the inter-dependence of the different areas as they affect the overall functioning of the school. This is particularly important for development planning which takes account of SEN where there is this inter-dependence. One way of dealing with this relatedness is to actively pursue SEN developments as both separate from other areas and as integral to them. However, it is possible to think of SEN school developments which are more distinctly about SEN and others which are more integral to other areas and aspects of a school's development.

Kinds of development

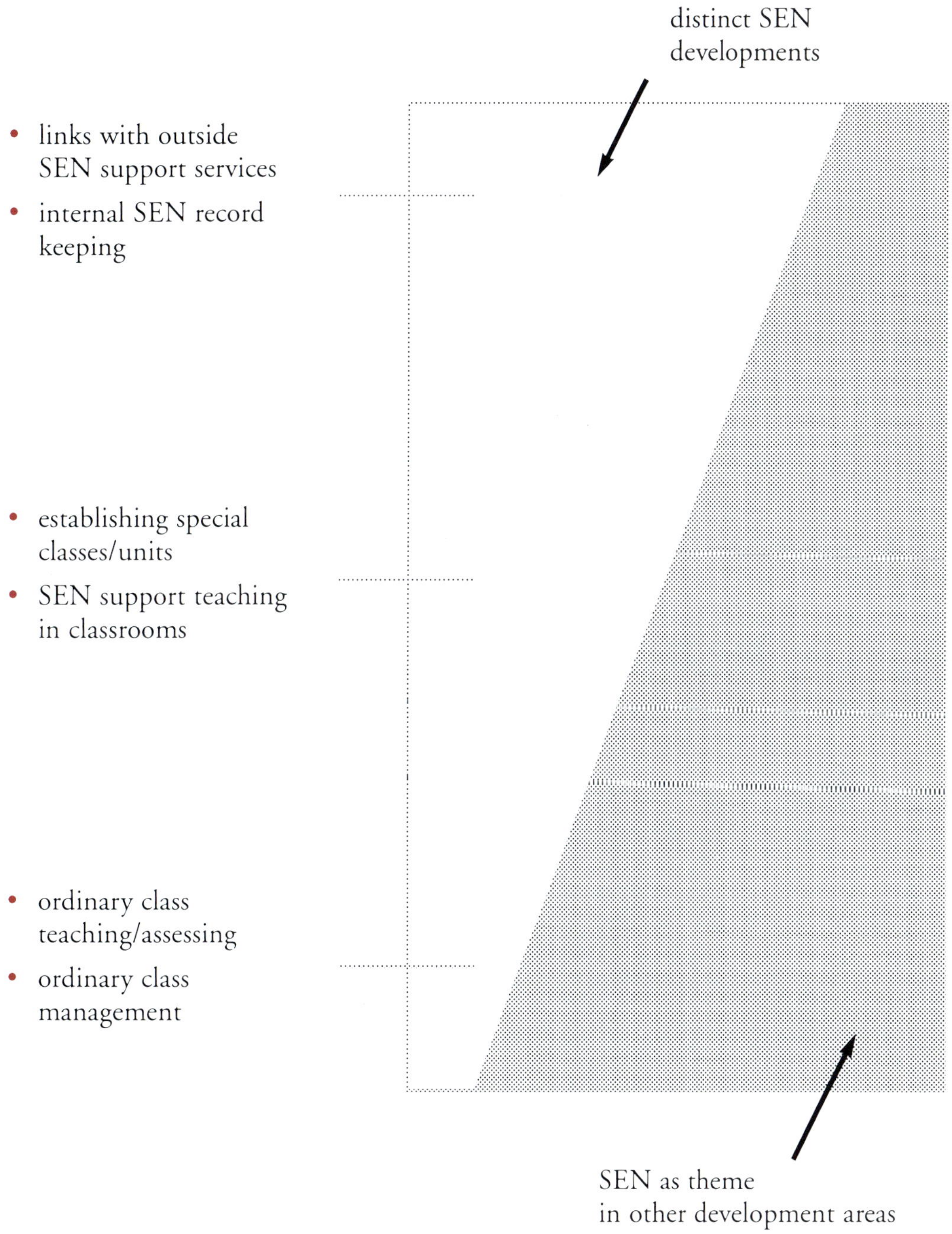

The figure above illustrates that some kinds of development can be seen as more distinctly concerned with SEN and can be undertaken as the main focus of a development. Other kinds of development relevant to SEN can be seen as integral to other areas of development. These form the range of development, but as the figure indicates distinct SEN developments also have some integral aspects, as integral aspects also have some distinct elements. Somewhere in the middle of this range are developments which have more of a balance between distinct and integral aspects.

Identifying distinct SEN developments and other developments with a SEN theme is not a fixed matter nor can these elements be separated in a definitive way. Nevertheless, it is useful to identify these elements as it enables planning from a SEN perspective to be mindful of realistic considerations about the way special educational needs is embedded in overall school activities.

SEN developments which are *mainly about* SEN concern the systems of recording and intervening using the school's own resources for the minority of pupils who need additional or different provision from what is available to others in the school. These developments also relate to the working relationships with outside support services, like the Educational Psychology service, and the initiation of statutory assessment. Developments in these areas can be undertaken as specific areas for improvements following the Code of Practice.

Other SEN developments which are more *integral to other developments* in the school are concerned with curriculum planning for ordinary classes, teaching and assessing for all where the emphasis is on adapting for individual differences in learning. The orientation here is that general planning and teaching take account of learner diversity in the way that teaching and learning is managed. SEN developments which are integral to other developments need to be considered as an important theme and systematically applied when these other areas are being reviewed and developed.

Much of the research on school improvement shows that change which is actively supported by the head teacher and senior management is more likely to fare well. The head's role is central because s/he can support the setting of shared goals amongst the staff members, establish procedures and structures to enable collaboration between different individuals and groups within the staff and set into motion the systems for monitoring the results. The importance of the senior management role applies especially to the area of SEN where there is a particular need for coordination of developments across the different areas of the school's work.

The approach to school development planning taken in this pack places particular importance on the need for the coordination of the SEN development planning to be undertaken by the senior management of the school.

The school's SEN policy and its school development plans

As discussed above, the requirement that schools have an SEN policy and that they report on it annually needs to be linked to the process of general development planning in schools.

The approach taken in this pack is that schools report their SEN policy after initiating and implementing a round of development planning. The school's SEN policy document will however be distinct from documents which contain details of the school's development plans. The school's published SEN policy will certainly need to refer to the school development plan and those aspects of SEN policy and practice which are scheduled in the plan. Schools will need to formulate written development plans, and staff will need to be involved in agreeing on the format of such a document.

Skelton, Reeves and Playfoot[2] suggest that the format for schools' development plans could be four to five pages at most. The plans are best presented simply and could include reference to:

- realistic targets;
- time and scale for change;
- definitions of responsibilities for the change process;
- resource and financial needs.

References

1 Fullan M G and Stiegelbauer (1991) *The New Meaning of Educational Change.* Cassell

2 Skelton M, Reeves G and Playfoot D (1991) *Development Planning for Primary Schools.* NFER-Nelson

The main review: questions to support school self-review

Contents

Introduction 45

The main review 47

Setting priorities for development 60

Introduction

The main aims of conducting the review are:

- to identify strengths and weaknesses in the school's SEN policy and practice;
- to identify areas for development;
- to set priorities amongst these areas for development;
- to help to relate SEN developments to other whole school developments in the school development plan.

There may be additional benefits from conducting the review, in terms of:

- initiating a debate on SEN in the school;
- engaging staff in the development process;
- highlighting shared views about SEN policy and practice and highlighting the areas where there are different views; and
- supporting the staff in reflecting on SEN policy and practice: their own and the school's.

This review document offers a series of questions that schools may want to ask of themselves in each area of their SEN policy and practice. The questions have been designed to help schools address some of the key issues in each area. They are not necessarily questions to which schools will have clear and immediate answers, rather they are questions that will help schools to probe for themselves the different areas of their work for pupils with SEN. The questions will help schools to examine each area of SEN policy and practice against the guidance of the Code of Practice, against the advice on schools' SEN policies, and in the context of other policies and practice in other areas of the school's endeavours.

Particularly to begin with there may be many questions to which schools will be saying 'We haven't got those,' 'We haven't done that' or 'We don't know.' The purpose of the questions is not to find schools wanting, but rather to help schools identify the areas where they will need to do some work and to support them in thinking about which of these areas may need to be addressed immediately and which can become medium or longer term priorities.

Equally the questions are not seen as being exhaustive and they may not provide precisely the focus that schools are seeking. The review questions can be taken and adapted by schools in the way that is most helpful to them. Some spaces have been left in each section for schools to add their own questions, and others, of course, can be omitted. Schools may find it helpful to adapt the questions in the light of using the review for the first time so that when they return to use it subsequently it may better fit their particular circumstances.

Schools will need to think carefully about how they use the review: as a whole staff, with everyone completing it; or using a steering group to guide the work, and drawing on the whole school or on particular staff, departments, or the wider community as necessary. In addition, the governors will need to give careful thought to the way in which they exercise oversight of this work. This might be assisted by governor representation on any steering group that may be established. These issues are discussed in more detail in the sections of this unit which look at: Organising the work in school, page 33 and: The governors and the school's SEN policy, page 29.

Schools will need to consider how the responses to the review are to be analysed, summarised and circulated.

The main review

Values and principles

Questions	Comments
1. What are the key principles which inform the school's provision for pupils with SEN?	
2. How widely are they known, understood and supported?	
3. Are these principles consistent with: • the principles underpinning the Code of Practice? • the LEA's policy on SEN? • the overall aims of the school?	
4. What broad objectives has the school set for its SEN policy?	
5. What arrangements are there for the implementation of the school's SEN policy?	

Identification and assessment and review

Questions	Comments
1. How does the school ensure that pupils' SEN are identified as early as possible?	
2. How is information on pupil achievement recorded and used in planning future learning?	
3. How does the school's approach to assessment, recording and reporting take account of pupils with SEN?	
4. How are arrangements for identifying and supporting pupils with emotional and behavioural difficulties coordinated with the school's whole approach to behaviour?	
5. In what ways are pupils themselves involved in the identification and assessment of their own SEN, the planning of support and the reviewing of their progress?	
6. Are all the staff aware of the procedures in the school for identifying and assessing pupils with SEN?	
7. What arrangements does the school make to review the progress of pupils with SEN?	
8. What arrangements does the school make for the annual review of pupils with a statement of SEN?	
9. Are the school's procedures consistent with: • the staged approach set out in the Code of Practice? • the LEA's policy on SEN?	

Access to the curriculum

Questions	Comments
1. How does the school ensure that all pupils have access to a broad and balanced curriculum including the National Curriculum?	
2. How does the school promote a range of teaching methods and learning activities that will enhance access to the curriculum for all pupils with SEN?	
3. How does the school make individual planning for pupils with SEN an integral part of curriculum planning for all children, when planning: • special help at stage 1? • individual education plans at stages 2 and 3? • targets for pupils with statements?	
4. How does the school promote a climate in which all teachers perceive it to be their responsibility to ensure that all pupils progress and achieve?	
5. How does the school support teachers in meeting the learning needs of all pupils?	
6. In what ways are pupils involved in the planning and implementation of any special arrangements to meet their learning needs?	
7. How does the school monitor the effectiveness of its curricular provision in terms of its impact on the quality of learning and standards of achievement for all pupils, including those with SEN?	

Roles and responsibilities

Questions	Comments
1. How does the school ensure that all the adults in the school understand their responsibilities to pupils with SEN?	
2. How do the special needs coordinator, the curriculum and pastoral leaders, and the senior management of the school support teachers in their responsibilities?	
3. Does the school have an agreed view of the specific SEN responsibilities of the: • governors? • head teacher? • SEN coordinator? • curriculum leaders? • pastoral leaders? • class/subject teachers?	
4. How does the school's description of roles and responsibilities compare with that set out in the Code?	

Staff development

Questions	Comments
1. How does the school identify and meet staff development needs in respect of SEN?	
2. How does the school's approach to staff development support staff in fulfilling their specific SEN responsibilities?	
3. How are the school's priorities for staff development in SEN related to general staff development priorities and to the school development plan?	
4. What opportunities are there for staff to learn from and with each other?	
5. How does the school draw on the LEA's support and training on SEN?	
6. What other agencies does the school draw on to support staff development in SEN?	

Admissions, facilities, specialisms and integration

Questions	Comments
1. How does the school ensure that its admission arrangements do not disadvantage children with SEN?	
2. Does the school have any specialist expertise, special facility, or special access arrangements that may benefit pupils with SEN?	
3. Do children who might make use of any specialism, special facility or access arrangements have any priority at admission?	
4. How does the school ensure that, so far as is reasonably practicable, all pupils with SEN engage in the activities of the school together with pupils who do not have SEN?	
5. How does the school deploy its resources in support of integrated provision?	

Allocation of resources

Questions	Comments
1. How does the school ensure that funding allocated to it, for the purpose of meeting the SEN of pupils, is used for that purpose?	
2. How much support is allocated to: • individual pupils? • in-class support? • pupil withdrawal? • teacher support? • curriculum support?	
3. What criteria are used in making this allocation of support?	
4. How does the school's allocation of resources for SEN reflect: • staff roles and responsibilities in respect of SEN? • level of need amongst different groups of pupils?	
5. How does the allocation of resources reflect: • the school's SEN values and principles? • SEN priorities within the school development plan?	
6. How does the school evaluate the effectiveness of its use of resources?	

Parent involvement

Questions	Comments
1. How does the school involve parents in the progress and development of their child at school?	
2. What opportunities are there for teachers and parents to share initial concerns about a child's progress?	
3. How are parents' views taken into account throughout the school-based stages of assessment and provision?	
4. How does the school plan to involve parents of children with a statement in statutory annual reviews?	
5. How can a parent register a complaint in respect of the provision for their child with SEN?	
6. What procedures does the school have for responding to a complaint by a parent in respect of the provision for their child with SEN?	
7. What information is made available to parents about special educational provision at the school, and in the LEA?	
8. What information is given to parents about sources of support that may be available to them at the school, or in the area?	

Support services and other schools

Questions	Comments
1. What use does the school make of support services to enhance its provision for pupils with SEN?	
2. How are support services used at the different stages of assessment and provision in particular, but not only, at stage 3?	
3. What assessment of its need for support services does the school make with the LEA?	
4. How are all staff informed about the way in which the school works with support services?	
5. How does the school consult with other schools to minimise duplication of effort and maximise efficient use of resources and expertise in meeting the SEN of pupils?	
6. Does the school currently share any SEN resources with other schools?	

Transfer and transition

(* denotes phase specific question)

Questions	Comments
1. What special arrangements are made at the transfer between phases for pupils with SEN?	
2. To what extent are these arrangements additional to or different from the arrangements for any pupil?	
3. *What arrangements has the school made to plan for the transition of young people with SEN to post-school provision?	
4. *What particular arrangements has the school made for the development of transition plans for young people with a statement in the light of the guidance in the Code?	

Working with other agencies

(*denotes phase specific question)

Questions	Comments
1. What arrangements exist at the school for linking with: • the educational welfare service? • the health service? • social services? • voluntary organisations?	
2. To what extent do the school's arrangements for linking with these agencies reflect those set out in the Code of Practice?	
3. How does the LEA support the development of school links with these agencies?	
4. What particular arrangements does the school make for linking with relevant agencies when a child with SEN is admitted to the school?	
5. *What particular arrangements does the school make with other agencies for the development of transition plans for young people with a statement?	

Monitoring and evaluation

Questions	Comments
1. What priorities has the school set for the development of its policy and practice on SEN?	
2. How does the school propose to monitor the implementation of its policy? What targets has the school set?	
3. How is the school planning to report on all the areas required of them in the Schools' SEN Policies Regulations? What arrangements need to be set in place?	
4. How far can the school demonstrate that it 'has regard to' the Code of Practice?	
5. What performance indicators does the school use to measure the effectiveness of its provision for pupils with SEN?	
6. How does the school propose to evaluate its policy against the broad principles and objectives set out at the beginning of its policy?	

Setting priorities for development

Summarising the outcome of the review

Following the review, the first task for the school will be to summarise the outcome so that the insights and the information gained can be used to good effect in planning the school's subsequent work.

The school may have involved a large number of people in responding to the review. The more who have been involved, the more information there will be to be analysed and summarised. However, whilst the involvement of a wide range of people in this exercise will create a more onerous task immediately, it may encourage the interest and commitment that will render the later stages of development and implementation more straight forward.

No matter how the school has conducted the review there will be a significant amount of information to be analysed and the school will need to consider carefully how this work is to be done. It will be important to have available a summary of the review:

- for all those who contributed to the review;
- as a resource for the school's reference, particularly when reporting on the implementation of the school's SEN policy in the annual report;
- to inform and direct the development work and to ensure that the focus of this work is on the areas that the school and the wider community consider the highest priority.

Where a consensus emerges about the school's special educational provision and about the priority areas for development, the school will have clear indications as to what they need to do next. Where significant differences emerge from amongst the views expressed, the school will need to analyse these differences.

Firstly, it will be important to analyse different views in terms of who is expressing them. So, for instance different views might be expressed by newly qualified teachers and more experienced colleagues, by teaching and non-teaching staff, by staff and the broader school community, by staff with more precise SEN responsibilities and those with more general SEN responsibilities, those with pastoral and those with curricular responsibilities.

There will need to be some further analysis to shed light on the reasons for the views being taken by different groups. All this information will need to be taken into account as the school sets its priorities for the next stage of the work.

There are three main questions that the school will need to address in planning the next stage:

- what are the priority development needs in SEN;
- how do these fit in with other priorities within the school development plan; and
- when and how are these SEN development needs going to be addressed?

What are the priority development needs in SEN?

The school may want to use sheet GD8 on page 86 of the support materials to list identified development needs.

In deciding what are the priority development needs in SEN there is a range of information that the school will want to consider. Sheet GD9 on page 87 of the support materials offers a summary of these.

The school has available to it all the information from the review. The review is constructed to take account of the new national framework of legislation and guidance, in particular Part III of the 1993 Act, the schools' SEN policy requirements and the Code of Practice. Thus, conducting the review gives the school the opportunity to consider their SEN policy and practice within this framework.

The school will also have available to it the outcome of any recent external evaluation by OFSTED, by the LEA or by other agencies. Such evaluation will have given the school clear indications about the priority SEN development needs. Where there is a recent evaluation to draw upon this will clearly inform the school's response to the review itself as well as setting SEN development priorities directly for the school. In addition, the school will have available a range of information on National Curriculum achievements, which, when analysed appropriately, will yield useful information about the progress of pupils with SEN. The school may have drawn upon such information in completing the review. If not, it would be appropriate to incorporate such information at this stage.

There will be a range of information from other forms of monitoring such as that from the monitoring of attendance. This may also inform the school's view of what the SEN development priorities should be.

The school will want to draw on this wide range of information when deciding what should be their order of SEN priorities: what constitutes an immediate, a medium-term and a longer term priority. These SEN priorities then need to be set in the context of other priorities within the school development plan.

How do SEN development needs fit in with other priorities within the school development plan?

SEN priorities will be linked more or less closely to other priorities that the school has set within its development plan, and the school will need to consider how these different priorities feed into and feed off one another.

So, for example, one of the existing priorities within the school development plan may be the school's policy on assessment. At the same time, the school may have identified assessment of pupils with SEN as an SEN development priority. In this case, the school will need to consider carefully at least three possible ways of dovetailing these priorities:

- the school might proceed with the work on the school's assessment policy and subsequently, in the light of that work, with the school's approach to assessment for pupils with SEN. The work on the assessment for pupils with SEN could thus be set firmly within the context of the school's approach to assessment for all pupils;
- the school might decide that the development work on both the general and the SEN assessment policy and practice should proceed at the same time since the two pieces of work are so intimately related they could feed off each other during the development period;
- the school might decide that the work on the assessment of pupils with SEN should proceed first, as a pilot study, and then the work in this area could inform the development of the school's approach to the assessment of all pupils.

Clearly, there will be a range of ways in which developments in different areas will be related to each other. It will not be solely a matter of the relationship between the school's policy and practice for all pupils and the school's policy and practice for pupils with SEN.

It may be, for instance, that the school is proposing to change from withdrawal to in-class support for bi-lingual learners, and that this may coincide with the school's decision to examine its approach to withdrawal or in-class support for pupils with SEN. In such a case the school might decide that these two developments should be linked. Equally, proposed curriculum development work in mathematics, for example, might be broadened to incorporate the development of access to the mathematics curriculum for pupils with SEN.

There is a number of ways in which development priorities for provision for pupils with SEN can sit alongside, feed into and feed off other priorities within the school development plan. The school will need to examine the balance of advantage of one approach over another, of one order over another.

When and how are SEN development needs going to be addressed?

Having decided on how SEN priorities should dovetail with other priorities within the school development plan, it will be important to set timescales against the work to be done. So, it will be important to indicate what work will be done on SEN next term, next year and thereafter.

The school may want to use sheet GD8 on page 86 of the support materials and set out how and when each identified development need is going to be met.

This information will need to be recorded within the school development plan but it will also be important in writing up the school's SEN policy. So for example, if the school's policy and practice on involving parents of children with SEN is considered to be a medium-term priority, then it will be important to say, within the policy, and following a summary of the school's current approach, that this area of the school's work is being reviewed, and to give the time-scale for that review.

The next section looks in more detail at how the school might write up its SEN policy.

Writing up the school's SEN policy

Contents

Introduction 65

What has to be in the school's SEN policy 67

Introduction

The Education (Special Educational Needs) (Information) Regulations 1994 came into effect on 1 September 1994. Circular 6/94, The Organisation of Special Educational Provision, indicates that schools should draw up their policies during 1994-1995 and the Regulations require schools to publish information about their policies by 1 August 1995. In the first annual report to parents published after 1 August 1995, and in all subsequent annual reports, schools are required to report on the implementation of their SEN policy. In addition, schools will be required to summarise their SEN policy in the school prospectus that they publish in 1995 for the 1996-97 school year, and in subsequent years.

Schools are required to publish information on 17 different elements within their SEN policy. This is summarised on sheet GD4, page 82 of the support materials, and is set out in full in the next section of this unit. The requirements for special schools and for special schools in hospitals are different and these are set out on sheets GD6 and GD7 respectively, on pages 84 and 85 of the support materials.

The published policy is for the information of those outside the school and therefore needs to present a summary of a few key points under each heading. Circular 6/94 sets out the issues that should be addressed. These are summarised in the next section of this unit, but schools will want to refer to the guidance itself before they draw up their policy.

Schools might consider setting out under each heading a paragraph or two summarising a few key principles and a few key points about their practice that epitomise the school's approach. For most elements within the policy this will mean a brief paragraph and no more than half a side of A4. For a few elements as much as a side of A4 might be needed. When the school has well developed policies in other areas for example on assessment or on behaviour, these may already incorporate much of the school's approach to pupils with SEN. Schools may want to refer to these other policies in their SEN policy perhaps picking out a few key points within those policies that apply in particular to pupils with SEN.

Where schools are using the approach advocated in this pack, they may want to indicate which elements of the policy they are proposing to review and develop within the coming year, and which will be included in the year after as well, where the school development plan is already agreed.

Circular 6/94 advises schools that their SEN policy:

> *'should be readily available to parents,'*

and that:

> *'some schools may wish to distribute copies of the policy to parents.'*

from paragraph 2, Circular 6/94

Schools will want to express their policies in language which makes them accessible to parents and a wider readership. Accessibility will also hinge on the policy being succinctly expressed. Some schools consult parents on their SEN policy. There will be considerable benefit to be derived from consulting parents and the wider community on both the content and style of the policy.

For the school's own use there will be a wealth of material that will need to accompany the SEN policy. This might include:

- more detailed description of the roles and responsibilities of different staff;
- copies of internal referral and record keeping forms;
- samples of individual education plans (IEPs);
- working documents that are part of the school's current review and development of SEN provision;
- a summary of the SEN elements in the school development plan;
- copies of other policies to which the SEN policy may refer; and
- other documents to which the school considers all staff may need to be able to refer.

This material can be kept together in a handbook available to all staff at the school.

What has to be in the school's SEN policy

This section sets out the 17 elements on which mainstream schools are required to report in their SEN policy. Under each heading there are:

- notes, based on the guidance in Circular 6/94 indicating the issues on which schools should report;
- references into the relevant paragraph(s) of Circular 6/94. Schools will want to refer to these for further guidance;
- references to the relevant unit in this pack. These references are in italics.

Following the section on the school's SEN policy there is comparable information about the requirements of the annual report. This sets out the requirements of the regulations, and, under each heading:

- reference to the information that should be included, based on the guidance in Circular 6/94; and
- reference to relevant units in this pack. These references are in italics.

The school's SEN policy

Basic information about the school's special educational provision:

1. The objectives of the governing body in making provision for pupils with SEN, and a description of how the governing body's SEN policy will contribute towards meeting those objectives.

Policy should include:

- guiding principles which inform provision;
- the objectives which the policy seeks to secure.

Guidance: paragraph 30 of Circular 6/94.

These issues are explored in Unit 2: Values and principles.

2. The name of the person who is responsible for coordinating the day-to-day provision of education for pupils with SEN at the school (whether or not the person is known as the SEN coordinator).

Policy should include:

- the name of the person responsible for coordinating SEN provision.

Guidance: paragraph 31 of Circular 6/94.

3. The arrangements which have been made for coordinating the provision of education for pupils with SEN at the school.

Policy should include:

- the role of the SEN coordinator or team as set out in the Code;
- the role of:
  - the governing body;
  - the head teacher;
  - any committee set up by the governors;
- how special educational provision is considered in the strategic management of the school.

Guidance: paragraphs 32 and 33 of Circular 6/94.

These issues are explored in Unit 5: Roles and responsibilities.

4. The admission arrangements for pupils with SEN who do not have a statement in so far as they differ from the arrangements for other pupils.

Policy should include:

- any priority given to children with SEN;
- criteria for such priority and information to be considered against criteria;
- any priority given to children who may make use of special facilities at the school.

Guidance: paragraphs 34 - 35 of Circular 6/94.

These issues are explored in Unit 7: Admissions, facilities, specialisms and integration.

5. The kinds of provision for SEN in which the school specialises and any special units.

Policy should include:

- any particular SEN in which the school has specialist experience or expertise;
- any special unit, and:
  - expertise of staff;
  - special equipment;
  - arrangements for support;
  - arrangements for integration.

Guidance: paragraph 36 of Circular 6/94.

These issues are explored in Unit 7: Admissions, facilities, specialisms and integration.

6. Facilities for pupils with SEN at the school including facilities which increase or assist access to the school by pupils who are disabled.

Policy should include:

- any special expertise;
- equipment, fixtures and fittings or characteristics of the school building;
- particular arrangements for access;

Guidance: paragraphs 37-39 of Circular 6/94.

These issues are explored in Unit 7: Admission, facilities, specialisms and integration.

Information about the school's policies for the identification, assessment and provision for all pupils with SEN:

7. How resources are allocated to and amongst pupils with SEN.

Policy should include:

- the principles governing the school's allocation of resources to and amongst pupils with SEN;
- how the governing body ensures that funds are used to help them meet pupils' SEN;
- where the school has delegated funds for pupils with statements, how the governing body allocates fund to ensure that the provision specified in statements is made.

Guidance: paragraphs 40-42 of Circular 6/94.

These issues are explored in Unit 8: Allocation of resources.

8. How pupils with SEN are identified and their needs determined and reviewed.

Policy should include:

- the school's identification, assessment, monitoring and review procedures;
- the staged procedures adopted by the school.

Guidance: paragraph 43 of Circular 6/94.

These issues are explored in Unit 3: Identification, assessment and review.

9. Arrangements for providing access by pupils with SEN to a balanced and broadly based curriculum (including the National Curriculum).

Policy should include:

- how the school will provide access to the curriculum. This may include:
  - general curriculum development;
  - the range of teaching strategies used;
  - the impact of support/withdrawal on access.

Guidance: paragraph 44 of Circular 6/94.

These issues are explored in Unit 4: Access to the curriculum.

10. How pupils with SEN engage in the activities of the school together with pupils who do not have SEN.

Policy should include:

- arrangements for integration of pupils with SEN with pupils who do not have SEN, including:
  - social integration, particularly if child is in a unit at the school;
  - integration in respect of work in all areas of the curriculum;
  - how rooms and buildings have been adapted to avoid segregation.

Guidance: paragraphs 45-47 of Circular 6/94.

These issues are explored in Unit 7: Admissions, facilities, specialisms and integration.

11. How the governing body evaluate the success of the education which is provided at the school to pupils with SEN.

Policy should include:

- how the school proposes to demonstrate the effective implementation of its policy;
- any specific targets against which the success of particular aspects of the policy can be measured.

Guidance: paragraph 48 of Circular 6/94.

These issues are explored in Unit 13: Monitoring and evaluation.

12. Any arrangements made by the governing body relating to the treatment of complaints from parents of pupils with SEN concerning the provision made at the school.

Policy should include:

- how parents can make a complaint about the special educational provision made for their child at the school;
- how that complaint will be dealt with;
- could include target times for responding.

Guidance: paragraph 49 of Circular 6/94.

These issues are explored in Unit 9: Parent involvement.

Information about the school's staffing policies and partnership with bodies beyond the school:

> 13. Any arrangements made by the governing body relating to in-service training for staff in relation to SEN.

Policy should include:

- plans for staff development;
- where appropriate policy to include needs of non-teaching assistants;
- any joint arrangements with other schools.

Guidance: paragraph 50 of Circular 6/94.

These issues are explored in Unit 6: Staff development.

> 14. The use made of teachers and facilities from outside the school including links with support services for SEN.

Policy should include:

- schools arrangements for access to external support services for pupils with SEN;
- the sources from which the school seeks external specialist support;
- any service level agreement with the LEA.

Guidance: paragraph 51 of Circular 6/94.

These issues are explored in Unit 10: Support services and other schools.

> 15. The role played by the parents of pupils with SEN.

Policy should include:

- arrangements for partnership with parents of children with SEN;
- how the school acts on parental concern;
- how parents are involved when a concern is expressed within the school;
- how parents' views are incorporated in assessment and review;
- how parents are fully informed about procedures in the school;
- how parents are made welcome in the school.

Guidance: paragraph 52 of Circular 6/94

These issues are explored in Unit 9: Parent involvement.

16. Any links with other schools, including special schools, and the provision made for the transition of pupils with SEN between schools or between the school and the next stage of life or education.

The policy should include:

- any arrangements whereby the school draws upon the staff and resources of other schools including special schools;
- any arrangements for integrating special school pupils in mainstream;
- any standing consultative arrangements with other schools;
- any arrangements to share resources and expertise.
- arrangements for supporting the transition of pupils between schools and to post-school arrangements.

Guidance: paragraphs 53 and 54 of Circular 6/94.

The issues on linking with other schools are explored in Unit 10: Support services and other schools.

The issues on transfer and transition are explored in Unit 11: Transfer and transition.

17. Links with health services, social services and educational welfare services and any voluntary organisations which work on behalf of children with SEN.

The policy should include:

- how the school works with:
  - the health service;
  - the social services department;
  - the education welfare service;
- any links with voluntary organisations;
- arrangements for liaison between SEN coordinator and the designated officers of:
  - the district health authority;
  - the social services department.

Guidance: paragraph 55 of Circular 6/94.

These issues are explored in Unit 12: Working with other agencies.

Information in annual report

Schedule 4 to the Education (Special Educational Needs) (Information) Regulations 1994 sets out the information which schools are required to give in their annual report. This is set out below.

Paragraphs 59-61 of Circular 6/94 provide guidance on this information.

1. The success of the governing body's SEN policies in the period since the last annual report.

The school must report on:

- the effectiveness of the implementation of their SEN policy.

The Code advises that the report should demonstrate the effectiveness of:

- the school's arrangements for the identification and assessment of pupils with SEN;
- the provision made for such pupils;
- the school's arrangements for monitoring and record-keeping;
- the school's use of external support services and agencies.

Circular 6/94 also alerts schools to the opportunity, in the report, to:

- assess the effectiveness of the policy against:
  - the broad principles and objectives set out in the policy;
  - the criteria set out in the section of the school SEN policy on monitoring and evaluation;
- alert parents to the availability of the policy.

Some of these issues are explored in Unit 13: Monitoring and evaluation. Other units contain relevant information, too.

2. Significant changes in the governing body's policy on pupils with SEN since the last annual report.

Report should include:

- any amendments made or proposed over the year;
- why made;
- how they will affect special educational provision:
  - at the school;
  - in the area served by the school.

Schools using this pack to review and develop their SEN policy will be able to refer to planned changes brought about through the development work.

3. The outcome of any consultation carried out under section 161(3) of the Education Act 1993.

The governing body may have consulted with other schools, the LEA and the Funding Agency for Schools (FAS) on some of the following:

- schools' SEN policies;
- maximising the use of expertise and equipment;
- developing a specialism;
- utilising support services;
- buildings adaptations;
- in-service teacher training;
- grant-maintained status.

Guidance on these points is set out in paragraph 90 of Circular 6/94.

Some of these issues are explored in Unit 10: Support services and other schools. Other units also contain relevant information.

4. How resources have been allocated to and amongst pupils with SEN since the last annual report.

Report should include:

- principles under which resources allocated to and amongst pupils with SEN over past year, might include for example:
  - deployment of teaching and non-teaching staff;
  - purchase of specialist equipment;

but need not take the form of a precise financial account.

These issues are explored in Unit 8: Allocation of resources.

Support materials

Contents

GD 1	Special educational needs: the definition in the 1993 Act	79
GD 2	The duties of governors in Part III of the Education Act, 1993	80
GD 3	Roles and responsibilities in mainstream schools	81
GD 4	Schools' SEN policies	82
GD 5	Annual report	83
GD 6	SEN policies: special schools	84
GD 7	Information from special schools in hospitals	85
GD 8	Setting priorities for development	86
GD 9	SEN priorities: what does the school need to consider?	87
GD 10	Schools' SEN policies pack: aims	88
GD 11	Schools' SEN policies pack: using the materials	89
GD 12	Schools' SEN policies pack: structure	90
GD 13	Schools' SEN policies pack: units in the pack	91
GD 14	Schools' SEN policies pack: what might a written policy look like?	92

Notes:

- The pages in this section may be photocopied.
- Many of the pages will benefit from being enlarged for use.
- The initials GD identify the support materials as belonging to this Unit: Guide to using the pack.

Special educational needs: the definition in the 1993 Act

A child has special educational needs if he or she has a learning difficulty which calls for special educational provision to be made for him or her.

A child has a learning difficulty if he or she:

(a) has a significantly greater difficulty in learning than the majority of children of the same age;

(b) has a disability which either prevents or hinders the child from making use of educational facilities of a kind provided for children of the same age in schools within the area of the local education authority;

(c) is under five and falls within the definition at (a) or (b) above or would do if special educational provision was not made for the child.

A child must not be regarded as having a learning difficulty solely because the language or form of language of the home is different from the language in which he or she is or will be taught.

Special educational provision means:

(a) for a child over two, educational provision which is additional to, or otherwise different from, the educational provision made generally for children of the child's age in maintained schools, other than special schools, in the area;

(b) for a child under two, educational provision of any kind.

Section 156

from: The Code of Practice

The duties of governors in Part III of the Education Act, 1993 GD2

Governing bodies of maintained mainstream schools must:

- do their best to secure that the necessary provision is made for any pupil who has SEN - 161(1)(a);
- secure that, where the head teacher or the appropriate governor has been informed by the LEA that a pupil has SEN, those needs are made known to all who are likely to teach him or her - 161(1)(b);
- secure that teachers in the school are aware of the importance of identifying, and providing for, those pupils who have SEN - 161(1)(c);
- when necessary or desirable in order to coordinate provision for pupils with SEN, consult the LEA, the FAS and the governing bodies of other schools - 161(3);
- ensure that the pupil joins in the activities of the school together with pupils who do not have SEN, so far as that is reasonably practical and compatible with the pupil receiving the necessary special educational provision, the efficient education of other children in the school and the efficient use of resources - 161(4);
- draw up and report annually to parents on their policy for pupils with special educational needs - 161(5);

Governing bodies exercising functions under Part III of the 1993 Act have to 'have regard to the provisions of the code'.

from: The Code of Practice

Roles and responsibilities in mainstream schools

Provision for pupils with SEN is a matter for the school as a whole. In addition to the governing body, the school's head teacher, SEN coordinator or team, and all other members of staff have important responsibilities. In practice the division of responsibility is a matter for individual schools, to be decided in the light of a school's circumstances and size, priorities and ethos. But schools should bear in mind the following:

- **the governing body** should, in cooperation with the head teacher, determine the school's general policy and approach to provision for children with SEN, establish the appropriate staffing and funding arrangements and maintain a general oversight of the school's work;
- **the governing body** may appoint a **committee** to take a particular interest in and closely monitor the school's work on behalf of children with SEN;
- **the head teacher** has responsibility for the day-to-day **management** of all aspects of the school's work, including provision for children with SEN. He or she will keep the governing body fully informed. At the same time, the head teacher will work closely with the school's SEN coordinator or team;
- the **SEN coordinator or team**, working closely with their fellow teachers, has responsibility for the day-to-day **operation** of the school's SEN policy and for coordinating provision for pupils with SEN, particularly at stages 2 and 3;
- all teaching and non-teaching staff should be involved in the development of the school's SEN policy and be fully aware of the school's procedures for identifying, assessing and making provision for pupils with SEN.

Whatever arrangements are made in a particular school, statutory duties remain with the governing body.

from: The Code of Practice

Schools' SEN policies

Basic information about the school's special educational provision:

- the objectives of the school's SEN policy;
- the name of the school's SEN coordinator or teacher responsible for the day-to-day operation of the SEN policy;
- the arrangements for coordinating educational provision for pupils with SEN;
- admission arrangements;
- any SEN specialism and any special units;
- any special facilities which increase or assist access to the school by pupils with SEN.

Information about the school's policies for identification, assessment and provision for all pupils with SEN:

- the allocation of resources to and amongst pupils with SEN;
- identification and assessment arrangements; and review procedures;
- arrangements for providing access for pupils with SEN to a balanced and broadly based curriculum, including the National Curriculum;
- how children with SEN are integrated within the school as a whole;
- criteria for evaluating the success of the school's SEN policy;
- arrangements for considering complaints about special educational provision within the school.

Information about the school's staffing policies and partnership with bodies beyond the school:

- the school's arrangements for SEN in-service training;
- use made of teachers and facilities from outside the school, including support services;
- arrangements for partnership with parents;
- links with other mainstream schools and special schools, including arrangements when pupils change schools or leave school;
- links with health and social services, educational welfare services and any voluntary organisations.

from: The Code of Practice

Annual report

The governing body's annual report must include information on:

- the success of the SEN policy;
- significant changes in the policy;
- any consultation with the LEA, the Funding Agency for Schools, and other schools;
- how resources have been allocated to and amongst children with SEN over the year.

baesd on: The Education (Special Educational Needs) (Information) Regulations 1994

Basic information about the school's special educational provision

1. The objectives of the governing body in making provision for pupils with SEN and a description of how the governing body's SEN policy will contribute towards meeting those objects.
2. The kinds of SEN for which provision is made at the school.
3. Facilities for pupils at the school including facilities which increase or assist access to the school by pupils who are disabled.

Information about the school's policies for the assessment and provision for all pupils with SEN

4. How resources are allocated amongst pupils.
5. How the needs of pupils are identified and reviewed.
6. Arrangements for providing access by pupils to a balanced and broadly based curriculum (including the National Curriculum).
7. How the governing body evaluate the success of the education which is provided at the school to pupils.
8. Any arrangements made by the governing body relating to the treatment of complaints from parents of pupils concerning the provision made at the school.

Information about the school's staffing policies and partnership with bodies beyond the school

9. Any arrangements made by the governing body relating to in-service training for staff in relation to SEN.
10. The use made of teachers and facilities from outside the school including links with support services for SEN.
11. The role played by parents of pupils.
12. Any links with other schools, and any arrangements for managing the transition of pupils between schools or between the school and the next stage of life or education.
13. Links with child health services, social services and educational welfare services and any voluntary organisations which work on behalf of children with SEN.

from: The Education (Special Educational Needs) (Information) Regulations 1994

Information from special schools in hospitals GD7

1. The name of the person who is responsible for coordinating the day to day provision of education for pupils with SEN at the school (whether or not the person is known as the SEN coordinator).

2. How pupils with SEN are identified and their needs determined and reviewed.

3. How resources are allocated to and amongst pupils with SEN.

4. How the educational progress of pupils with SEN is monitored.

5. How the contents of a pupil's statement are ascertained and made known to staff.

6. The arrangements for ensuring continuity of the educational provision set out in a pupil's statement differentiating where necessary between long stay and short stay patients.

7. Arrangements for providing access by pupils with SEN to a balanced and broadly based curriculum.

8. The use made of teachers and facilities from outside the school including links with support services for SEN.

from: The Education (Special Educational Needs) (Information) Regulations 1994

Setting priorities for development

GD8

Identified SEN development needs	How will each development need be addressed	When?

SEN priorities: what does the school need to consider?

Framework

- National framework, in particular:
  - Code of Practice;
  - Regulations and guidance on School's SEN policies;
- LEA framework:
  - LEA's SEN policy;
  - LEA curriculum statement;
  - LEA's information on SEN procedures.

Evaluation

- any recent external evaluation OFSTED inspection/LEA inspection;
- information from monitoring:
  - National Curriculum achievements;
  - attendance;
- Views of:
  - teachers;
  - parents;
  - pupils;
  - governors;
  - support staff;
  - any outside agencies the school may wish to consult (EPs, EWOs, Special Schools, Support Services, PRUs' voluntary organisations including those run by and for disabled people).

Information

- reports to the governing body by the staff;
- existing documentation by the school:
  - SEN policy;
  - other policies, for example, behaviour, equal opportunities, curriculum policy documents;
  - school development plan;
  - school mission statement;
  - school handbook.

The pack aims to:

- support schools in writing up their SEN policy in line with the requirements of Regulations;
- help schools 'have regard to' the Code;
- be of continuing use to schools in reviewing and developing their SEN policy and practice;
- provide a framework for setting SEN priorities within the context of the school's development plan.

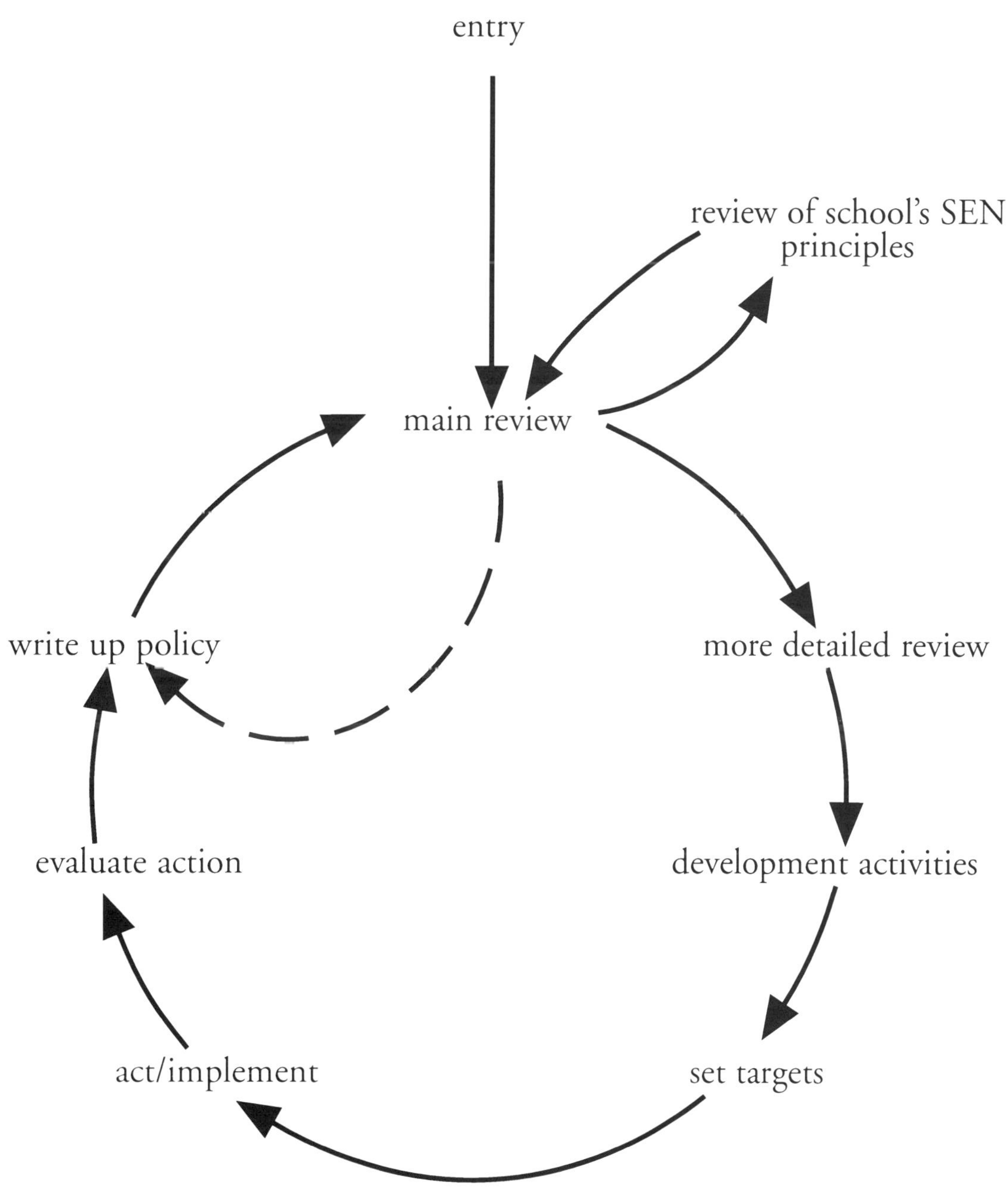
entry
review of school's SEN principles
main review
write up policy
more detailed review
evaluate action
development activities
act/implement
set targets

Schools' SEN policies pack: structure

The pack provides schools with:

- a main review document;
- a set of units each of which provides:
  - a more detailed review document, in each of the areas of the school's SEN policy and practice;
  - a range of staff development activities;
  - materials to support the development activities;
  - reference to other supportive documents;
- guidance on writing up the school's policy to meet the requirements of the Regulations;
- guidance to governors on the development of the school's SEN policy;
- a collection of discussion papers.

Unit 1: Guide to using the pack;

Units 2-13 address different areas of the school's SEN policy:

2: Values and principles;
3: Identification, assessment and review;
4: Access to the curriculum;
5: Roles and responsibilities;
6: Staff development;
7: Admissions, facilities, specialisms and integration;
8: Allocation of resources;
9: Parent involvement;
10: Support services and other schools;
11: Transfer and transition;
12: Working with other agencies;
13: Monitoring and evaluation;

Unit 14: Summary of contents;

Discussion papers in a series of five companion volumes.

What might a written policy look like?

Considerations:

- 17 elements;
- audience;
- practicalities:

  - a paragraph on each area;
  - principles and key aspects of practice;
  - may indicate elements of policy to be reviewed and developed next year;

- supporting materials in staff handbook;
- school development plans.

Further reading

Guide to using the pack

Further reading

School development planning

Abbott R and others (1988) *GRIDS School Handbooks. 2nd edition,* Primary and Secondary versions. Longman for the SCDC

Department of Education and Science (1989) *School Development Plans Project, 1: planning for school development: advice for governors, headteachers and teachers.* HMSO

Department of Education and Science (1991) *School Development Plans Project, 2: development Planning: a practical guide: advice to governors, headteachers and teachers.* HMSO

Hargreaves D H and Hopkins D (1991) *The Empowered School: the management and practice of development planning.* Cassell

HM Inspector of Schools/Scottish Office Education Department (1992) *Using Ethos Indicators Secondary School Self-Evaluation: taking account of the views of pupils, parents and teachers: School Development Planning - Support materials.* HM Inspector of Schools/SOED

National framework

Allen L (ed) (1994) *ACE Special Education Handbook.* Advisory Centre for Education

Audit Commission/HMI (1992) *Getting in on the Act: provision for pupils with Special Educational Needs: The National Picture.* HMSO

Audit Commission/HMI (1992) *Getting the Act Together: provision for pupils with special educational needs: a management handbook for schools and local education authorities.* HMSO

Audit Commission/HMI (1994) *The Act Moves On: progress in special educational needs.* Audit Commission bulletin, November 1994. HMSO

Bentley A, Russell P and Stobbs P (1994) *An Agenda for Action.* National Children's Bureau

Department of Education and Science (1978) *Special Educational Needs: report of the Committee of Enquiry into the Education of Handicapped Children and Young People (The Warnock Report).* HMSO

Goacher B, Evans J, Welton J and Wedell K (1988) *The 1981 Education Act: policy and provision for special educational needs.* Cassell

University of London Institute of Education, National Children's Bureau and Oxford Polytechnic (1989) *Decision-making for Special Educational Needs: an inter-service resource pack.* The 1981 Act: Research Dissemination and Management Development Project. Tecmedia Limited

Directions in special educational needs

Ainscow M (ed) (1991) *Effective Schools for All.* Fulton

Ashdown R, Carpenter B and Bovair K (ed) (1991) *The Curriculum Challenge.* Falmer

Booth T, Swann W, Masterton M and Potts P (eds) (1992) *Curricula for Diversity in Education.* The Open University/Routledge.

Bovair K, Carpenter B and Upton G (1993) *Special Curricula Needs.* Fulton

Dessent T (1987) *Making the Ordinary School Special.* Falmer

Dyson A and Gains C (eds) (1993) *Special Education Towards the Year 2,000.* Fulton

Inner London Education Authority (1985) *Educational Opportunities for All? Report of the committee reviewing provision to meet special educational needs, chaired by Mr John Fish.* ILEA

National Commission on Education (1993) *Briefings.* Heinemann

National Commission on Education (1993) *Learning to Succeed: a radical look at education today and a strategy for the future.* Heinemann

Visser J and Upton G (1993) *Special Education in Britain after Warnock.* Fulton

Walters B (1994) *Management for Special Needs.* Cassell

Schools' SEN policies

Bines H (1993) Whole school policies in the new era, *British Journal of Special Education* 10,3, 91-94

Moss G (1994) Policy and practice, *Special Children Issue* 76, June/July 1994. In subsequent issues of *Special Children,* Geoff Moss edits a series on 'Managing Special Needs in Mainstream Schools' (Autumn 1994)

Oldham Education Department (1991) *Guidelines for Reviewing Special Needs Policy and Practice in Secondary Schools.* Quality Development Branch, Oldham

Palmer C, Redfern R and Smith K (1994) The four Ps of policy, *British Journal of Special Education,* 21, 1, 4-6

Designed for governors

Advisory Centre for Education (1994) *Governors and Special Needs,* ACE information sheet. ACE, Unit 1B, Aberdeen Studios, 22 Highbury Grove, London N5 2EA

Rogers R (1995) *ACE Governors' Handbook.* ACE

Institute of School and College Governors (1994) *Check Lists for Governors.* ISCG, Avondale Park School, Sirdar Road, London W11 4EE

Scott L (1993) *Governors and Special Needs: report of an enquiry into governor training for SEN.* Advisory Centre for Education

Scott L (1993) *Special Needs - Support for Governors: guidance and training materials to help school governors carry out their duties for SEN.* Advisory Centre for Education

Ulrich W (1994) Policy must be published: New responsibilities for special needs, in *NAGM News.* Issue: 6. National Association for Governors and Managers (NAGM) 21, Bennetts Hill, Birmingham B2 5QP

Waterman C (1993) *Finding Your Way Around the 1993 Education Act: with implications for governors, heads and LEAs.* Action for Governors Information and Training (AGIT) Lyng Hall, Blackberry Lane, Coventry, CV2 3JS

There are also two useful references at the end of the section on SEN and school development planning, page 41.